A Date With Destiny

DAVID A. MARSHALL

authorHOUSE

AuthorHouse™
1663 Liberty Drive
Bloomington, IN 47403
www.authorhouse.com
Phone: 833-262-8899

© 2022 David A. Marshall. All rights reserved.

No part of this book may be reproduced, stored in a retrieval system, or transmitted by any means without the written permission of the author.

Published by AuthorHouse   06/13/2022

ISBN: 978-1-6655-6252-2 (sc)
ISBN: 978-1-6655-6253-9 (e)

Library of Congress Control Number: 2022911256

Print information available on the last page.

Any people depicted in stock imagery provided by Getty Images are models, and such images are being used for illustrative purposes only.
Certain stock imagery © Getty Images.

This book is printed on acid-free paper.

Because of the dynamic nature of the Internet, any web addresses or links contained in this book may have changed since publication and may no longer be valid. The views expressed in this work are solely those of the author and do not necessarily reflect the views of the publisher, and the publisher hereby disclaims any responsibility for them.

Dedication

This book is dedicated in memory of
my mother, Susie Etta Marshall
She was my greatest inspiration

Contents

Foreword xi
Acknowledgements xiii
There Was A Time xv
Testimonies xvii
To My Readers xix

I cherish moments with U 1
The Couple 3
Infatuation 4
Your Picture 5
The Things I love About You 6
We 8
U So Cool 9
My Cellular Love 10
The Mask 11
Afternoon Scent AAA 12
Beauty (A sonnet in love) 13
Destiny 14
Bad Sandy 15
Chicken 17
Action Speaks louder Than Words 19
A Passing Antecedent 20
Falling In Love 21
Finding The Right Voice To This Poem 22
First Love 23
Gambling Phenomena 24
Game of Life 25
Glory 26
Habit Forming 27
Happy Poem 28
I Am 29
I get high off YOU 30

I left my heart	31
I once was a Poem	32
Journey	33
Just be Real	34
Just Imagine	35
Justice	36
King Darius	37
King of Pop	39
Life Is Too Much With Us	41
Lost	42
Love	43
Morning Bliss	44
Never	45
Obama the big Comeback	46
OBP	48
Out of touch with Reality	49
Prince	50
Record Man & More	52
Diagnosis Poetry	54
Shhhhh-for a Moment	55
Sonnet In Motion	56
Sounds 1	58
The Changing Scenes of Life	60
The Best	61
The Destroyer	63
The Indefatigable Freedom Fighter	65
The King & Company	67
The Marshall Doctrine	69
The Spirit In Your Voice	71
The Unequaled Air Jordan	72
The Wanderer	74
Tomorrow Is Another Day	76
Violence Eradicated	77
Waiting	79
Wheel of life	80
Write A Poem For Me	82

Dreaming Plus	83
Incomparable Poet	84
Operation HOPE Poem	86
Godfather of Soul	88
IT (Coronavirus)	90
BJ	92
Mrs. G	94
That Special Day	95
The Dancer Becomes The Poet	96
Remembering Ferguson	97
Unborn Poem	98
Soundless Tracks	99
Babe	100
A Misunderstanding	101
Free	102
The Thought Revisited	103
Biden –Build Back Better	104
The Beautiful Lady In The Subway	106
We Are People 2	108
Words	110
I Have Seen Blacks at Work	111
Cameron's Ponds	113
About the Author	115

Foreword

From an honorable mention in his first book, VOICES OF REALITY, published in 2009, I am honored to reintroduce you to poet-extraordinaire, David A. Marshall, a soon to be best-selling author.

In this book of poetry, Dave masterfully assembled some of his greatest works. It is a masterful collection of thought provoking messages on a wide-ranging number of topics both personal and worldly. As in his past writings, the poet challenges your comfort zone. This leads to a more introspective look at the essence of the subject matter. Dave sees the world not through the superficial lens of conventional mores but through the prism of its refined essence. He is searching for the truth and brings you along on the journey. Always concerned about the human condition, your enlightenment is his goal. He artfully writes about emotional dilemmas involving love, aspirations and frustrations. Addressing issues of social consciousness and interaction is also of great concern to the poet.

I have known Dave Marshall for more than forty years. We have experience a lot over the years. But through all the trials and tribulations of life, Dave remains optimistic about the future including the pivotal role romantic love plays in our life. He is both inspirational and aspirational.

David A. Marshall is not just a poet but the poet we need!

EDDIE L. RIVENS MBA, CPA

Acknowledgements

I would like to thank my sovereign God again for giving me the energy and creative Spirit to bring forth this project. In retrospect, I would like to thank Fairfax Landstreet, who went on to be with the Lord Years ago. His strong persistence voice of encouragement and inspiration remain frozen in my mind Today. I also would like to thank all of the contributors for their time and efforts in help bringing This book to fruition. I would like to thank the great staff at Author house especially Eve Carson and Melanie Lear for their outstanding assistance. I owe a debt of gratitude to Edward Rivens for his extraordinary talents in help synthesizing Everything. A big time thanks to Charmaine Gibbs for her unwavering longevity support, and profound Affinity for my work. She once told me that she wants to read every word I write. A world of gratitude to Shakur Afrikanus, the great Harlem historian, for his unparalleled Encouragement and strong moral support.

There Was A Time

I remember so fondly the short (but seemed long as a child) walk to the little red house With my brothers Stuart and John, my sister Lilly and Cousin Marion, to go see David and Them, to eat Pet's big white homemade biscuits from the coal-fired stove, sit on the porch And play, around the little red house, around the farm in South Carolina. David Marshall was Like a big brother, maybe more like a good cousin, hanging out, hiking around, playing ball on the farm. Seven miles from York. Too far to go to town. Hot summers. Running in races. Digging a small swimming pool/pond. Feeding pigs. Just hanging out. David was well respected In our family. Everyone had something nice to say about him. Moving to New York but coming To SC for visits. I lost touch when I went to college.

My mother gave us his news and news of Etta, His elegant mom. When I got an invitation last year to come and hear David's reading of his poetry, I was overjoyed. My husband Howard and I were both so honored to hear his poems and those Of the other poets and the music accompanying the poetry. To meet his dynamic daughter. Unforgettable. I am so lucky.

Eleanor Landstreet J.D.

As far back as I can recall, my Dad was always writing songs and poems. We would be chatting, and suddenly he would say an idea for a poem just arrived In my mind for a new poem. Thus, another poem was born. His new book contains a lot of intoxicating poems. I have many favorites, but among my favorites are "king of Pop", "U so cool", "King Darius", and "Sonnet in Motion". After reading this book, I think the reader will further understand his profound passion for the Written word, and his concerns for the social situations that continue to plague us daily

Tori Dudley

Testimonies

I hold in high regard the friendship of David Marshall. Must be at least 18 years now since We first met. And such a pleasure indeed. I have literally watched David's growth with his poetry Writing. Kudos to his first book "Voices of Reality" and now "Destiny". Please read and enjoy this diversified body of work that has been meticulously selected and Drafted out so we the readers can play with, cry to and be inspired by.

Maria Chisolm-Poetess Author of Sudan's Angels

As you read poetry of David Marshall you will find that each one has awakened a different emotion. Some are funny and you laugh, some are sad and you cry. Regardless, the one fact is that all are Enlightening and life impacting. Every one of his poems is wrapped in creative brilliance so that you Are filled with anticipation until you read the next.

Karleyne Joiner

David Marshall is one of the most soulful, authentic poets of our day. He emotionally and Spiritually engages and inspires the reader with each syllable. David compassionately instills his Incredible heart and his passion into his work and is an inspiration for all.

Mary Ehrsam
President
Operation HOPE 1 Partnerships

To My Readers

I went deep into the ethers of my mind and as a consequence these poems were born.

I hope you enjoy perusing them as much as I profoundly relished writing them.

Keep in mind that I continue to write just for YOU.

So take a deep breath and relax as I welcome you into my world of Poetry.

                              Blessings,
                         David A. Marshall

I cherish moments with U

Now there is nothing else I would rather do than to cherish moments with U

When I met you my entire world was falling apart
But since you have walked into my life, you have given my engine a brand new start
When we are out and having a good time nothing else seems to occupy my mind
Baby when we are out and enjoying the town; I am so into to you that it seems
Like no one else is around

When we are not together my whole world is so empty and blue
I just can't wait to see you again, because I cherish those sweet moments with U

You know when we are out and having fun, it seems like our souls are attached together
And it feels like we are combined into one

Baby when I am with you I wish I could freeze the moments and time
Because when you are away romantic thoughts of you linger constantly on my mind

I cherish moments with U sweet moments with U just lovable unforgettable
Moments with U

I honestly want us to grow closer together, because I just adore all of the sweet things
That you do

You are the radiant sunshine in my life, and I truly cherish moments with you
When we are together it just seems like time travels so fast
I am looking for a stable and meaningful relationship---one that is really going to last

I cherish each microsecond with U

Baby I just cherish each wonderful heartfelt moment with U

The Couple

I felt happiness and stability in the air as the bus landed at its desired location they embarked from the bus embraced in a fashion that the world's greatest dictionary could not explain

They tightly held on to each other dismissing the cacophony in the surrounding atmosphere you could discern the accumulated bliss in their liaison saturated over the years by the strange dampness in the air

As the rain swirled around from east to west, they were not concerned about tomorrow they were self-absorbed in the happiness they shared at that very moment they had seen a million laughs—they had heard a thousand stories—they had seen a flood of tears, but the love they had consummated over the passage of time was unequaled and had no competition

When you saw them, you saw happiness—when you saw them you discerned commitment when you saw them, you saw a connective tissue that will never be separated if you travel all over this global universe-it will take a gargantuan effort to ascertain a love that will equal or surpass what they have birthed and accomplished together

Life will move onward changing destinations and directions based on different variables, but the love they have nurtured, protected, and admired will only grow as the seconds become years

When you start on your journey you will notice the clouds in your mind---the rain falling from the sky—devastations in parts of the world—fierce debates over how economic challenges should be resolved, but rest assure from the cortex of your brain through it all, they will HAVE and BE together FOREVER

Infatuation

I saw the flowers swimming together when I heard the deep echo
Of your matchless voice
Overwhelmed by the sensation of my emotions, I was attracted to the
Sight and sound of a feeling that swept up my deep desire of my
imagination
I was tossing and turning in a river of romance that was difficult to
separate from reality
So beautiful—so sweet, I was lost in the light and sunbeams of your
Charismatic sex appeal
As I was grappling with a thought that my feelings would wane, suddenly
an overpowering ebullition spirit smothered the thirst of my emotions
I felt trapped within myself and could not release myself
Just like an unpredictable torrent snowstorm, I was soaked in curiosity
by your infinite intellect
Just like being hooked on drugs, cigarettes, and alcohol- I had become
addicted to it
When it happened and why it happened, I was lost for an explanation
Lured by your love and scent, I was completely caught off guard by your
Ambitions and supercilious demeanor
I was enamored and held spellbound by the mystery of you
I was grappling with a deep emotion that was making love to itself, when
in reality it was a figment of my imagination depicted in a romance film
starring Humphrey Bogart
Minutes travel to years as my mind fluttered around the thought of you
Being seduced by someone from your past
I tried hard but could not find a rudder to help combat this emotional
Roller coaster
Something will happen the next second in this world, but just like a
voiceless
Grave at midnight, I still will be surrounded by the spirit of your beauty

Your Picture

I look at you and it's difficult to unravel all the feelings that exist
Melancholy and forlorn situations might try to overwhelm me, but when
I look at you a beautiful resurrection brings out the best in my feelings
You are silent as warm air, but you have a towering effect on my
Personality
We communicate in proximity although you may be
Scattered miles away
Oh, your picture it's almost a substitute for the natural you
When I look at you, I am inspired, energized and motivated by your
actions beyond your deepest imagination
Your picture—your picture your beauty thy see
When I look at you—it brings out the best in me
When I look at you, I can smell the beauty of your perfume and feel the
Presence of your unconditional love
Although you are stationary --you move mountains when I stare into
Your picturesque eyes and hear that sensuous voice
When I see you, I discern a thousand stories told and a plethora of
Triumph experiences
If I did not see it or touch it, I would be like a lost needle in a crowded jungle
When I look at you, I receive the strongest vibration that you are looking
Deep into the storehouse of my soul
If you are near –my universe is saturated with extroverted happiness
everywhere
When I mull about you, I receive the greatest stimulus package ever
Assembled
Oh, sweet Picture-Oh sweet unforgettable picture-your beauty thy see
Your picture your beauty thy see
When I look at you – it brings out the very BEST in me

The Things I love About You

I love your eyes, because they tell me a pregnant story that I have never perused before

I love your vivacious intellectual conversation, because it makes my super ego yield endless traits

I love your superfluous divine walk, because it depicts to me that rare beauty that is stationary within

I love your smile, because it is unique and tells me that your ideas are packed with extraordinary power

I love your body, because it is enviable, it is enthralling, it is unique, and it keeps my ego sharp and enriches my memory to the greatest highest threshold

I love the exotic way you kiss, because the warm taste I receive is so smooth and everlasting, until the rhythm in my body never forgets our strong interpersonal liaison

I love the way you make love, because it is sensational, and your delicate touch keeps my nerves in unison

You excite my whole body with profound memories, until my Id and Ego seem to have a party in another milieu

I love your philanthropic ways, because they vividly depict that caring love is still in this world

I love your deep embedded spirit, because it makes me remain close to my omnipresent Creator

You do things in such a prolific unique manner, until your diverse trademarks will be left throughout my body dancing and singing sweet melodies to each other

I love things about you, because you steadily remain just YOU

I just love your attributes

We

We walked together in love and harmony
Dismissing the sands in the universe

We talked in unison in a style that kept the rhythm in our relationship
On course for a perfect landing

On a pathway that never diverted from the deep turmoil of a haunted
Destination—we never lost that desire to relinquish our moral obligations

We grew in strength and determination to seal the destiny of our dreams
Our committed faith did not have to walk around searching for a long-lost dream

Things tried to vanish before our eyes caught up with life's staggering events
The rallying cry of the disturbances really solidified the absence of nature's
Craving for unjustifiable preoccupation

There is never no long thought or vicarious reminiscing
because we never have to concern ourselves with who we have been kissing

We vividly remember all the tangible things that brought us together
Losing those things is not a realistic reality in the bare soul of our fiber

Our inner testimonies spoke volumes of unconditional feelings

We are together as ONE

U So Cool

It was a torrid day in December
You were so cool so unflappable how could I not remember
I took another look to locate you on Facebook
Like to get to know you and maybe we could commence a history
Cause in the back of my mind you are just a floating mystery
They tell me you don't use drugs, smoke or drink
Like two lovers together-the way you use your vocabulary really make
Me think
You have a punctilious attitude and personality
I bet the world you can separate myth from reality
You are so articulate- I admire the way you walk and dress
Just like water turns to ice-you have made me alter my attire-
This I must confess
You are a rare specimen you are so cool
When I ponder deep into your conversation- I can tell you live
By the golden rule
If I were rich, I would buy you the moon and luminous stars above
But since I am not –I can shower U to death with respect and love
I could love you more –never love U less
If I could enter your world –there would never be room for loneliness
Teach me, bribe me, thrill me add and multiply Power and Pride
If we coalesce, we could re write the record books marching side by side
When I see U ---you make me feel so proud
You know how to distance yourself and interface with the right crowd
I see you my heart leaps through my eyes
When I contemplate all facets of life- the more you awaken my spirit
and make me realize
I tried to limit my desire-but your phraseology set my world on fire
Your style and equanimity are rated high among the best
You are so unflappable so cool U conspicuously stands out from the rest
U are sooooooooooooooooooooooooCOOL

My Cellular Love

Just like thirsty dry land crying out for water, they are hooked
Burning with anticipation, they just can't wait for another day to expose itself
They can't wait to ascertain what is unraveling in cyber space
It has reached a point that it has become extremely difficult for many to live without it
It's a conspicuous reality that has captured the minds and souls of the masses
Just look at them riding the subways, sitting on the bus, crossing the street they are tuned in
They are caught up in a frenzy of excitement, when they are having a love affair on twitter, Facebook, YouTube, Instagram and other media outlets
As a result of the ubiquitous penchant for their Cellular love, organic human contact is quickly
Losing its potency
It has great attributes, but has become a transparent compulsion for many
It's a graphic reality that more time is consumed looking down than ahead
I hear voices saying "My Cellular love –my cellular love you are nearly as great as the wondrous
Stars above"
You can see it in their eyes that some are addicted
You can hear it in their voices it is becoming an obsession
You can tell by the sounds of their footsteps that their prized instrument is the pride
And joy of their lives
Cellular love, cellular love – people are so fascinated with their Cellular love
They won't let you enter their own private universe, because many are held hostage
And hypnotized by the information and happiness that it reveals
In the background of my consciousness, I hear voices loudly saying "My Cellular love-
My Cellular love- I would be lost without you.
If it were suddenly taken away, many would be grappling with an enormous psychological shock
BUZZZZZZZ did someone just say its time for an upgrade??

The Mask

Have you been honest with yourself, or have you been concealing dangerous
Landmines within contents of your soul
It is written all over your countenance
It is revealed when you have an intimate discourse with others
Its strangling nearly choking you to the face of death, but you are still trying
To hold on to it

Its time to bring to light another metamorphosis
The Mask of pride must be revealed
You must let the world see and understand the real you
Don't let it hold you hostage
Unwrap that aged old candy bar that's been dormant so long
Stop camouflaging your identity
Step out from that shell of loneliness and self-pity into an environment
You have often dreamed about
Walk away from that clandestine world of fornication, jealously, infidelity,
Self-controlling and other transgressions

We need to see that special you that God created you to be
Let those dark clouds evaporate into a spirit of God's expectations
Don't let the realities of yesterday swallow up your lofty ambitions for today
Look into the mirror of your soul and ask yourself "what am I concealing
What is rupturing away the core of my consciousness"

Keep in mind that when you let go and let God your mind, body, and
Spirit will never want to hide, when you seriously uncover the Mask of pride

As the days continue to float away into the mysterious air of the unknown,
Stop disgracing your inherent feeling and seek wisdom as the steppingstone
In your life

Afternoon Scent AAA

I passed by our favorite place and memories almost swallowed me up
I saw your special chair wishing you were sitting in it
All the faces were the same, but really were not, because you were missing
I could still smell your powerful fragrance although it's been so long
I sat there and enjoyed our favorite brunch alone reminiscing
They played our best loved song, and tears in my eyes turned to ice
They danced to our favorite song, and my heart rhythm changed to bliss
Conversations in the air further proved that your absence will be difficult to surmount

Before the evening comes, I will look back on the afternoon and remember You

Beauty (A sonnet in love)

I see your beauteous, inquisitive eyes dissecting my body
Even when you are absence, your presence has an over powerful
Impact on the equilibrium of my heart rate

I hear you walking in the footsteps of my soul, as the impatient wind
Swirl up against the backdrop of my most intimate feelings

Like a hall of fame basketball, we bounce up and down in the rhythm of love,
When our ideas coalesce together

We make magnificent music together, when the cells in our universe unravel
Clandestine areas that were once invisible

Destiny

As I think about the creation of this universe
As I contemplate about the glorious stars in the sky
As I ponder about the laughing sounds of human nature
As I wash out yesterday and like a radar focus on tomorrow
I still believe in the awesome power of YOU

You had seen and had experienced so much
I have seen and experienced just as much
Through all those eerie days and nights, we still had hope and faith
Because of the present high-tech age, there is no stopping us now
Activities in the global universe were transparent and were making their
Own connections

In the background of our moral consciousness, we had heard floating through the
Air that it was impossible to happen
We had no control over the situation, but based on our own deep-rooted hubris
Nothing could circumvent our feelings from developing
We had heard from the mighty "Voice of Reality" and what was once so distance
Was now in proximity

The bells of the earth are now ringing out bliss and joy
Those old painful tears are disappearing into a world of oblivion

It had brought other folks together
It had made believers out of non-believers

As a result of old man Time, it has happened for and to us
It is more than magic---it's surreal

The seeds have been planted and now we can enjoy the fruits of our labor
My mind is unraveling a million thoughts and I have reached a destination

Yes, yes, it was you DESTINY that cohesively linked us together

Bad Sandy

There was a hush in the atmosphere unraveling an effect that was not present before
folks had talked about hurricanes hugo, katrina, irene and the subsequent devastation they had caused
my name was mentioned and the possible ramifications sent chills running through the veins
of the people residing in the north east
people were praying and thought i was going to turn and go in another direction
but when i did not, they froze in terror

When I decided to gain momentum, I brought along my relatives
Folks saw torrential rain and frightening, damaging winds up to 100 miles per hours
I was given a name, they called me "Sandy"
Before I made my landfall, folks were told to vacate their homes
A lot of them did not listen and ultimately paid grave consequences

My panorama of destruction was far and wide
The Northeast and several key States had never faced such devastation
I changed folks standard of living
People started to conflate like never before
Television and Radio shows were saturated with new about me

I slammed into the world's biggest renowned cities and created an environment of havoc
And cataclysms
Before you could blink an eye, I shut down big New York City
I closed down the Subway system, bridges, Schools and tunnels

People experienced hardships, suffering, grief, and agony that were beyond compare
They called me "Sandy"
The affluent and the less fortunate had no answer for me

I challenged people to display affection and generosity in ways that was contemplated before

During my reign of terror, I made chaos and pandemonium compete for the Gold Medal
As my might and power commenced to wane, folks started rebuilding a new chapter in their lives

My aftermath will be profoundly felt and talked about long after I have vanished
There will probably be other hurricanes in the future, but when folks mentioned "Sandy", you
Can bet they shall think about me

They called me "Sandy"

Chicken

He fascinated large crowds everywhere before DR J arrived on the scene
He played with boundless energy with prolific results long before Air Jordan nearly rewrote the record books

He was simply called "Chicken"

In his own social milieu and during his Era no one- I mean no one was equipped and armed with his overall basketball skills and abilities

He was so spectacular that he almost replaced Phenomenal in the dictionary
His shots were as deadly as a Cobra's bite and his extraordinary confidence had no equal

He wrote the record books in terms of the now so called three-point basket

His avid fans were spellbound, transfixed and was caught up in a state of paroxysm of excitement when they saw him perform
Playing with such killer instinct, his opponents never wanted to challenge or face him
Everybody admired and talked about him and could not really digest and swallow how great he was at such a young tender age

His defensive skills almost matched his offensive prowess

Yes, before DR J, MJ, and LBJ there was "Chicken"

His long fade away mesmerizing jump shot was a gargantuan testimony that will never be duplicated

His vainglorious temperament drove the fans into sheer ecstasy while displaying his on-court acumen

Due to life's vicissitudes and other phantasmagoric events that transpired in his life, the global universe did not have the opportunity to truly discern a basketball talent that will never exist again
Great players will continue to come and leave their own legacies
But just as sure as the weather will change from season to season

There will never be another "CHICKEN"

Action Speaks louder Than Words

Wait a minute, wait a minute everything you tell me sounds so sweet
But if you put some action into it, you would make everything complete
I've been going with you for a long time
Those beautiful words, those soft words have been blowing my mind

You say one thing, but you do something else
When I need you the most, you leave me all by my self
Think about it, you better think about it - baby haven't you heard
That action speaks louder than words
What you say and do can go a long way
But if you put some action into words, you can start a love
Revolution the very same day

Talk is cheap and can Easily be done
But if you prove your love to me, life can be so much fun

You tell me you can swim the ocean with your feet and only one hand
But if you prove it to me, then I will truly understand
Baby just don't sit there and say what you are going to do
I want to see results, then I will know it's true
From time to time you exhibit some peculiar ways
You become extremely silent, and I don't hear from you for days

Its almost old as time, and you probably have heard
Action oh action speaks louder than words

A Passing Antecedent

There were times when he wanted to advance but couldn't
The years were too tender, and wisdom had not reached its fruition
If only he had known what an animated conversation could produce—then

Sometimes reservation is a costly exercise
Others many others were ultimately responsible for him not discovering the
Truth
Oh, how he inherently wished that the empty times would have been
filled with
Tender loving warmth and breath-taking vapor
The competition of love sometimes leaves a cold heart unplugging artery

He sketched in his mind the perennial love affair that was just a mirage

Thoughts suddenly disseminated in every conceivable direction, and he had
Another senseless cup of coffee

The closing of the eyes and the opening of a better tomorrow constipated
his heart with a breath of translucent sunshine

Falling In Love

It started with that compatible smile and breath-taking look in your eyes
There was that unforgettable, inimitable kiss
I felt it metastasizing through every cell of my body
Feelings were developing that were beyond our control
Our minds said that it was the time
Our hearts corroborated that decision
When we touched- the thrill and power of imagination consolidated
Our feelings into one soul spirit
There was that inescapable chemistry that was not present before
You may try to suppress your feelings
You may try to put off reality until tomorrow
But when its time-nothing in this universe will circumvent it from happening
With all of your might- you will try to ignore it
But just like your shadow –you cannot erase it
We tried to fight it, but we both had to succumb
When your lips and eyes meet it feel like your heart is beating a
Thousand beats a minute
One of the greatest and most powerful feeling on this earth is the feeling
Of Falling in love
Your heart and mind begin to dance together in unison
Your imagination is beginning to run away from your thoughts
You can't wait to receive that text message
You are dying to hear that voice –so excited to see that face
I had heard a thousand voices speak
I had discovered a blissful emotion that was beyond compare
Felt like the stars had fallen from the sky
The rhythm in my soul was pumping petroleum purified oil
Just like quicksand swallowing your body into a whirlwind of excitement
You just can't stop it, because you are falling in love

Finding The Right Voice To This Poem

The cadence, rhythm, And the echo of silence are not working in total equilibrium

Grappling with a title that is out of sync, but needs to be on a harmonious road to a
Fruitful destination
Trying to surmount a rupture that is spreading at an almost record pace

Will it be about Destiny, Love, Desire, perseverance or just an albatross of black molasses
Wrapped around your satin DOLL

Will it be an ocean falling off the precipice of unwavering love

Will it be about a liberated Love Child searching for that profound inherent feeling of fantasy

Will it be about that narcissistic male messaging his bloated ego to placate that thirsty
Embedded demon

Will it outline a togetherness that should have been installed when the application of human
Nature was first created

Will it be a resounding voice shouting out the novel technological components that have this
Universe transfixed into an avaricious reality

I am still pondering, mulling and energetically itching to locate the Voice to this Poem

First Love

We were both younger than age itself
I found it difficult to create a conversation

You were as beautiful as life
Night after night I would romance you in my dreams
I even concealed my feelings from you and my friends

I was in love with love not knowing what the true meaning of what love really was

Once we made eye contact, I knew the feelings were real
I was an introvert and you were an extrovert
It did not matter, because the opportunity never presented itself

We never embraced and our lips never met
I often wondered what it would have been like to really get to know you

Digging deep, searching hard and finally realizing that sometimes
The First Love is the only true Love

Gambling Phenomena

As the people toss and turn and sometimes dance to their own rhythm, they are seriously contemplating about what tomorrow will bring

Just as certain as darkness turns to light, they will be anxious and itching to partake in their most serious deeply embedded social activity

They think, contemplate, ponder and mull when MS lady luck will open up the floodgate for some sort of financial blessing

They try all kinds of sorting schemes trying to hit their favorite numbers
Some rely on dreams, and past year patterns and trends
Some folks partake daily, while other gamble when they feel the impulse
Others depend mainly on highly intricate mathematical formulas

The old, the young and people from all levels of educational attainment find inherent satisfaction when they are gambling

They try numbers, scratch offs, slots. Blackjack, lotto games and anything else that arouses and stimulates their imagination

Some partake for the sport of it and sheer curiosity

Others partake because they have become addicted to it

Just as sure as the gambling game remain in existence someone somewhere will still be trying to beat the Game of Chance

Game of Life

We are all in the game of life but what's paramount is how well you stay inside and play by its rules
He had experienced setbacks, rejections, criticisms, unimaginable life Challenges, but his unwavering spirit did not succumb to those dangerous landmines
His body and spirit embedded a prize only he could win
At times the dark clouds in human nature tried to impede his progress
But he refused to give up
The torrent of landmines tossed in his direction were almost unbearable
He is still in the game---the game of life
The game can be cruel, cold, unfair, deadly faceless like a poem without an alphabet
The game is ongoing played and won by the most fortunate player
Her innate spirit told her she could win
It had eaten and swallowed up those alive who were vulnerable and insecure and did not take the game serious
She had suffered pain of love that had almost drowned out her happiness
She had been down and out in NYC and hunger had nearly split open her intestines

She still believed and rejoiced in the sanctuary of her spirit
The sun is going to shine—rain will fall among the wondrous stars above
The impatient wind will be felt but not seen
Her body embedded a prize only she could win
She was still in the game- the challenging game of life
Their survival skills were tested but they prevailed
I am resilient— I am striving to stay afloat
In the dawn hours of the sun set old Triton may blow his wretched horn in sweet harmony
Proteus may again rise from the deep blue sea of your brain
But just as long as you breathe—as long as your heart beats one more time –you will without question be partaking in this global deep dish salad bowl called the Game of life

Glory

Glory reach out and let the sunshine deeply into my window
Feel free to disregard all the selfish traits of humanity

Uplift me so that the waves of the sea will discern with enormous devices

Make the greatest human respond to me with great earthy mountains

Glory-change the color of all eyes so feasible solutions can be accomplished
You can make plausible relevant details revolve in a rather gregarious moment

Glory make my demeanor feel elements that my system never knew were present

Search for all the great beyond that were liberated in the kindness of all mankind

Without any prolong changes depleted horizons shall keep you safe guarded in all phantasmagoric revelations of life

Habit Forming

Just like an additive drug when it enters your vein
I can't stop loving you- I want to make love to you again and again
You make me feel so good, when you make sweet love to me
I never want to let you go, because sexually you make happy as I can be

Baby your love is habit forming- your sweet love is habit foaming
Every day my love for you just keeps growing and growing
Just like a medication, after taking it for so long you can't do without it
I am so much in love with you, in my dreams I just shout about it
Every time you make love to me I feel the impact of your love
I feel the rain, sun, moon, stars and everything else from above

Just like a narcotic your love is habit forming
Just like being addicted to alcohol, I am addicted to your love
I will never broach the idea of loving no other than you
Your love has such a hold on me, until there isn't nothing I would not do

You are the only one I want to cherish all the time
Because no one else could alter my mind

Just like cigarette smoking – your love is habit forming
Just like gambling its habit forming
Yes, indeed your love is habit forming
I can't seem to wiggle myself away from you
You have me doing things I normally don't do

Because your love is habit forming
Ooh your love is habit forming
Baby your love is habit forming

My love for you just keeps growing and growing

Happy Poem

They called me the Happy Poem, because I am never sad or in a melancholy mood
I take one day at a time and never worry about tomorrow, because I know tomorrow will take care of itself

They talk about me and even try to ridicule me, but it doesn't bother me, because my positive attitude remains the same

My heart and soul are so filled with joy and happiness; I don't have the time to be sad and blue

How can I be sad when I have my Most High always by my side leading and driving me in the right direction

Now search your mind, heart and soul and digest the contents of this message

So, when you are feeling blue, turn your thoughts on the Happy Poem and you will be happy too

I Am

I am the doorknob to your soul
I am the love that you have been seeking

I am the missing link to your puzzle
I am the sugar that makes your ideas sweet

I am the candle that lights your spirit up
I am the words that increase your vocabulary

I am the pen that forces you to write
I am the energy that causes you to sustain

I am who and what you want me to be

I am ------------------------------

I get high off YOU

Now I don't need no alcoholic beverages to stimulate my mind
Just a sniff of natures fresh air makes me think about you all the time
I don't need no drugs, because drugs don't turn me on
All I need is a night with you-I know we can write our own song

I wouldn't get no satisfaction by drugging myself away
But I will get a life time of fulfillment having your romantic affection every day
I love all the sweet things that you do
I get an automatic high when I think about you
Being with you made me a winner and I could never accept defeat
Baby since I've been with you – you have made my life complete

You make me stand and feel so proud by every little thing you do
Even when you are not present – I get automatically high off you
Instead of concentrating on drugs, I spend all my time thinking about you
Because your love is the best prescription and more than enough to see me through

I don't need an on-looker witness, because everything I say is true
Just believe firmly in me, when I tell you I get so high off you
I don't need no whiskey or wine
Just thinking about your personality, I get mighty high all the time
You turn me on in every little thing that you do
We make beautiful music together- I relish spending time with you

You are my alcohol and drugs all wrapped up together
I can tell by the look in your searching eyes our love will last forever

I get high off you
I just get so high off YOU

I left my heart

I left my heart inside of you a long time ago
I wondered off into the dark valley of the unknown

I tried desperately to connect to another soul, but I could not keep up
With the equilibrium in my mind

I left my heart in a place that was so secured that only love would be the
Deciding factor
I left my heart at a time that thoughts and ideas were so connected together
I tried laboriously to replace something that did not have an end to the puzzle

As I stumbled on different edges of society, I was uplifted by a vivid
dream deferred
Based on empirical feelings, I left my heart inside of you

My mind became overwhelmed by a desire that was trying to make
waves with a
Feeling that was never born

As I ponder deeply into the evolution of my tears, I discovered that I left
my heart in the right place

I left my heart in a world of bliss and optimism
I left my heart in a world that would not be challenged

I left my heart inside of YOU a long time ago

I once was a Poem

I used make people laugh and cry
I used to make folks tremble with excitement

I used to make others shake their heads for hours trying to understand me
I made people call on me when they were Down and Out

I made people fall in love just by thinking of me
I was no one special---just a Poem
I used to stop traffic in the middle of Time Square in New York

I used to make people smile when they were filled with anger
I used to make people think when they did not have a reason

I had the ability to turn words into a melody with the blink of an eye
I have made people conflate under mysterious circumstances
I made folks think of me when they were in the mood for making LOVE

I have been called a plethora of names with different faces

But through it all----------------I once was a POEM

Journey

I hear the melody and the sweet touching music in your voice when we are
On our destination
I see the beautiful sunshine written all over your healthy countenance

When you walk in your world, I feel and see the deep spirit in your body language
We will be held tightly together, because of what we birthed at the beginning

Along the way there may be disappointments, setbacks, nefarious remarks, but
We will surmount those challenges
We will not let outside forces disturb the rhythm in our spirits

We seriously care about the sadness in life, but greatly appreciate the laughter
In this universe
You are the air that I breathe and the light that turns my switch

As we enjoy and celebrate each other, we will experience the goodness of life

When we are with each other, we experience a cohesiveness that was invisible
Before
We are on our way and our world will be like the sub aqueous stillness of the Great renowned sea

This is and shall be our JOURNEY alone

Just be Real

I stay home every single night
Maintaining my commitment to do right

I believe in you and maintain all of my trust in you
I hear the bells in my heart telling me that we will never part

I don't care what they say, because I know that we can make a way
We must not be separated from each other
We made a promise that we must stick together regardless of the circumstances

Our love is strong and I know it will last
Because we will bury all of the secret memories of our past

We will sacrifice for each other's happiness
We will not worry about all of the rest

I think we are cognizant of how we really feel

It's about Love and Life and we must make everything real
The right package, the right prescription----it must be REAL

Just Imagine

Just imagine I would look up and there was not a cloud in the sky
I look around and I do not hear a voice in the atmosphere
I search my heart and soul and I cannot arrive at a profound feeling

The competition and the new world order have abandoned each other
The tears and the laughter have gone astray to a destination that will be
Revealed when forces coalesce
Footsteps of reality will leave an indelible impression when the moon drops
Decide to take a vacation

Desire, hope, faith and love will be lost in our vocabularies
Time and place and the rhythm of the universe will be cemented forever

I cannot wake up and IMAGINE a world without being with YOU

Justice

You soothe me with a satisfaction that a dictionary cannot explain

You enlighten my brain from the timetable of your energy

We communicate in such a random fashion, until my arteries reveal great liabilities
The touch of your warm watermelon excites the top of my honeymoon

Justice, in the middle of our destination, you just keep on thrilling my inherent secrets
The method you use is so everlasting, until I discern the sun professing at midnight

If you weren't alive and keeping me elated, I would be lost in a world of the great beyond
There is really no definition of you

Periodically, you express one in the highlights of your petition

I cannot erase you from the top of my ego and the gregarious world out there knows we profoundly need each other

Justice, Justice, You will always be what's happening

King Darius

For my son

I could not depict the frisson in the atmosphere during that unforgettable day
I was so excited and overwhelmed by the reality of you being born
I felt emotions that never existed before
It had taken nine months, and I wondered what you felt during that time
Were you anxious, apprehensive, excited about becoming a member of the Population?

As quick as a flash of lighting, you had expired
I reached out for help, but no one was there
I felt a shaking in my spirit—I felt a trembling in my heart
Just like that the world had stopped
Loss for words, I had no answer and I did not ask why it had happened
I was not in control---my most High was in charge
Flash back---flash back
Just to look at you-touch you for those precious moments cannot be described
In human terminology
When I looked at your countenance, I saw ambition
Your smile brought tears to my soul
Your heart was beating to the sound of a greater tomorrow
Oh how I weep for Darius
I cried silently "Darius come back son", but it was a wasted laborious endeavor
It felt like most of my vital statistics had stopped functioning
I was praying that it was only a bad dream
A vivid reverie revealed the two of us were playing baseball together
My most heartfelt dream was the two of us praying and praising God together
I walk around and I discern the face of another person, and I contemplate would
You look like him
I listen and I hear another unique voice, and I wonder would you sound like that

Since you have gone on to be with your creator, the world has changed significantly
The world has gone high tech crazy
Oh yes son you do have a sibling
She is tall, intelligent, and beautiful and has been blessed with a creative talent
That is beyond compare
Flashing through my mind like sweltering heat on an August day is what would you have become---a Lawyer, Doctor or may be a Poet—It would not have mattered as long as God was first place in your life
Darius I weep for you----oh Darius I weep for you
We love you
I can't see you, but I am cognizant of the reality that you are omnipresent
Just by thinking of you, I have the power to make it through another unpredictable DAY

King of Pop

When he arrived on the scene, he quickly showcased a talent at his age that
Simply overshadowed and buried his peers
At an early age, he worked laboriously to hone his singing and dancing skills that
Ultimately catapulted him to the top of his field

He captivated and held the world hostage with his ubiquitous astute pirouette
Movement highlighted in matchless video creations
Others tried to duplicate his unique video creative success, but fell conspicuously short

As human nature speaks to us via of storms and hurricanes, he set worldwide attendance
Records all over this planet mesmerizing fans into a paroxysmal of unmatched excitement

Each new CD he released set the universe on fire with peerless lyricism and unrivaled song improvisation
When he was seen in concert, fans were spellbound, awestruck and some succumbed to multiple orgasms as he performed his creative version of the famed "Moonwalk"

Regardless of all the record setting awards, fame and fortune his
Philanthropic endeavors
Excelled far beyond the norm

Playing to sell out venues and screaming adoring fans all over this celestial sphere, the
Unrivaled entertainer continued to display boundless energy and matchless creativity through
His final days
Rewinding the clock back to that special anniversary night, the King of Pop exhibited the

"Moonwalk" dance on TV that still have folks mesmerized and hypnotized in a state of
Unimaginable frenzy
With such Herculean classics as "Billy Jean", "Beat it", "Thriller"," Bad", "Don't stop until you
Get enough", "Black and White", the Mega star left a track record of accomplishments that will
Unlikely be surpassed
He moon walked his way into superstardom in a fashion that will never be duplicated again

We had the King of Rock and Roll, King of Rap, King of Soul, king of Country and Western, but
When the universe speaks from its heart and soul and spells out the title King of Pop-it will
Without a challenge say Michael Jackson

Life Is Too Much With Us

At times this life is too much with us past and present
Crying and laughing- praying and thinking, we find it difficult to
Surrender our power
Much do we realize that Time is melting away life this very hour

It feels that sometimes our world is sinking in quicksand
We are letting fears starve to death our happiness and love
Our mental equilibrium is falling on the precipice of loneliness and
Disappointments

We are carrying life's problems on our shoulders when the true realities
Have floated away into the galaxy among the beautiful stars above

We see the horrors of life sometimes transpire among the raindrops in the
Clouds and smiling sunshine rattling around the wondrous sounds of
human nature
We hear the sea storms in our minds
We feel the hurricanes in our hearts and discern the mighty wind
holding off
Unrivaled testimonies like a sordid boon

I tell you this life is too much with us sometimes past and present
We are times choked and strangled by our own blood, sweat and tears
Sometimes almost paralyzed by those highly charged emotions and
clandestine fears
Trying to digest the realities of life, we sometimes get swallowed up by others
Expectations and desires
life is too much with us past and present and there are times we find it difficult
to transfer our power

little oh little as we investigate the naked face of reality and contemplate—
what do we truly own in this planet that is really ours?
life –life is too much with us past and Present

Lost

I am trying hard to grab on to reality
Trying to find a world that has gone naked cold

Cannot make sense of the situation
You left without a scintilla of notice
I held you high in esteem and was always faithful
I am so confused, because I thought we had it all together

After how I feel about you, I probably will never love again
Like a broken mirror, I was crushed when I ascertained you were promiscuous
I thought love was real, but now I have doubts

Just like they say love is kind, but it is also blind

I have to shake the monster "Bewildered" which engulfs me, and with the Omnipresent help from my Problem Solver gain a foothold on reality

Love

I see your beautiful smile shinning against my pathway to success
You uplift me into your own television dreams

At times you shade my thoughts with tremendous associations

You have made the hairs on my pastor divide into separate paths

Without love, I would still be searching for the great unknown

You have made me cheerful when the earth was changing colors

Yet you have made me vapid when you weren't living up to your means

You have changed a lot of hearts over the vanishing years
Oh love you have made miracles shed a few tears

The nearness of you have separated millions of homes

At times you joke and smile
In contrast, you have made life not so worthwhile
One will never know where you came from
At times you have been seen sitting on a throne

I guess I will continue to search for your new knowledge
I will keep on trying to figure what makes you communicate

Love, oh Love tell me what makes you tick
Love, why are you such a mystery??????

Morning Bliss

I woke up with a feeling that I cannot describe
I see your lovingly face even though you are not present
I hear your voice even though you are miles away in distance
But you are omnipresent in my heart

I can't wait to tackle the day and all of its challenges
My concupiscence for you is deeper than the deep blue sea
This feeling only comes once in a lifetime and I am elated you are the primary reason

My coffee and breakfast travel through my system with prolific happiness
I can almost touch you by the scent of your sensuous fragrance
I could search this whole spacious world and could never replace this feeling

This morning what you have left is unique and will never be duplicated

Never

I will never say no to love
I will never say no to the butter flies I feel dancing in my heart

I see life all wrapped around your wonder sky when I experience the
Happiness in your voice
I will never say no to love when setbacks and disappointments try to
Become soul mates

I will never say no to love when it seems like things are murky or at the
Crossroads

The earth can rumble with curiosity and I will still never say no to love
Voices may yell out in tears and bliss
Voices may say turn around, but I will never say no to love

I will never say no to love even if I see a different story depicted in your eyes
Regardless of the circumstances – I will never say no

It will not be in my vocabulary to say no to your LOVE
It's not in my spirit to say no to your profound committed LOVE

Obama the big Comeback

When you announced that you were going to run for a 2nd term there were those who
Said your chance of winning was slim to none.

You had seen and had accomplished so much during your first term that through your eyes
You inherently knew that you would be victorious at the end
Those on the right said it was impossible for you to win—they said the deficit was too deep
They said too many folks were receiving entitlement benefits
They hollered out that the unemployment rate was too high
Embedded in the back of your mind you knew you would triumph again
Your challenger was vacillating all over the place on key issues
You did not waver ---your charismatic style and equanimity attitude were matchless
You synthesize a ground coalition that was prolific and unrivalled
Your pundits were saturating the air waves saying "it's going to be a land slide"

After the first debate, a lot of people vociferously said you were finished
Others said you were incompetent
You aggressively reached back into the sanctuary of your soul and overwhelmed your
Opponent in the following debates
Your command of the key issues domestically and internationally should be highlighted in
The politics Hall of Fame
As election day was approaching, the right said you would not win the swing states
They tried all sorts of schemes to circumvent you from winning
Just like a roaring lion that only motivated you to be more energized and resilient
After the big snowstorm landed with its results, you demonstrated salient leadership and compassion that will be admired and talked about for decades to come

As the polls were starting to close, your pundits were choking with laughter saying that it was
Going to be a land slide favoring your opponent
You were unflappable and your self-esteem was high as the sky
Suddenly there was a hush in the air--- then it happened
Just like a bomb exploding boom - you had been reelected President again
Those on the right started drowning in a quicksand of disappointment
Your headquarters were filled with pandemonium and bliss

What some had vividly stated would never happen had happened in a cyclopean fashion
History had once again been made and what a Comeback it was

Obama! Obama! The big Comeback

OBP

Chills splatter up and down my spine, when I contemplated your renowned greatness
When I first invaded your territory, I was overwhelmed by your spacious appearance

Diverse players came to you from contrasting geographical locations to further exhibit
And hone their overall skills
I visited you many times and you brought out the very best in my athletic endowments
As a result of you, I was able to attain enormous athletic success
As a result of you, I was able to garner a plethora of honors

Just for being there, we achieved tremendous accolades as a team
I still hear the big roar of the crowd every time I would wallop a signature home run
Fans were wildly excited to frequent you, because they knew they would be entertained
By some of the best players in the universe

I often dream about you seriously wishing I could turn back the hands of time
Still fantasizing about competing with the best

You are still there with a slight change in your countenance still attracting a wide
Array of talent from different paths of life

Old Ball Park memories of you and results remain buried deep in my mind
Old Ball Park thanks for being there when it really mattered

Out of touch with Reality

I 'm out of touch with reality
I' m out of touch with reality
Trying to face a world that has become extremely cloudy to me

Now I don't know my A B C's
And I don't know my 1 2 3 's

When you left me, my whole world came tumbling down
I see people daily, but I don't know that they are around
I used to have a master's degree
I used to have a P.H.D., but since you exited from my world
They don't mean nothing to me

I'm out of touch with reality so out of touch with reality
Come on back baby and help me get myself together
When its sunny outside it just seems like we are having bad weather

When people talk to me, I can't comprehend what they are saying
My world is in a state of chaos baby you got me praying
When someone speaks to me, it seems like he is speaking a foreign
Language from out of space
Baby you are messing with my mind, I feel like I don't belong to the human race
I' out of touch with reality
Trying to understand a world that is somewhat oblivious to me
I've forgotten what Biology all was about
I've forgotten what Psychology all was about
I tell you I've forgotten what Sociology all was about
Come on back baby, because you are the only one who really understands me
Ooh out of touch with reality
Trying to understand a world that has become very murky to me

Prince

From the moment he wiggled out of his mother's womb, he wanted to be a musician
Deep down in his soul, he wanted to play on the big stage
He worked laboriously to create his own style and mastered playing every conceivable
Instrument at a young tender age
Just like a new day opens its eyes to a plethora of challenges, he exploded into the
Entertainment atmosphere

His awesome acting talents was depicted in his runaway protean movie "Purple Rain".
Once people gleaned he was starring in the movie, they flocked to see him in record
Numbers
He set the universe on fire with a monster best selling album by the same name
He was called Prince
He dropped a torrent of albums in a short period of time working his way to superstardom
He was at the apex of his world, when he was making love to his guitar on stage
On stage, he displayed unparalleled showmanship teasing and bringing the roar of the
Crowd to an uncontrolled orgasm
During the zenith of his career, he gave us everything from a musical sphere Rock, Pop
And Soul
He was a musical genius and his business acumen had no equal
He was spiritual oriented and had profound affection for the underserved
His philanthropic behavior should be a role model we all should emulate
He loved singing and dancing and writing songs was his life
He inhaled and exhaled music

With such cyclopean classics as "When doves Cry", "Let's Go Crazy", "Purple Rain",
"1999", "Little Red Corvette", "The Most Beautiful Girl in The World" and others,
The multi-talented singer left songs that will be embedded in our memories forever

When all things are gathered together and the pantheon of the world's greatest
Entertainers are cemented in posterity, you won't have to turn many pages, because
"Prince" Rogers Nelson will be highlighted there

Record Man & More

As darkness fades away into the bright sunshine, you will find him there
Six days a week 10 hours a day, regardless of what's happening in the
Milieu, he will be there
Cars dashing in all directions- voices challenging each other in a vivacious
Interlocution, the world will find him there
If your musical interest expands greater than the big blue sea, he will placate
Your hungry heart
His awesome display of albums will go unchallenged
His collection of books has no equal

Call him the Record man & more sometime singing and dancing in unison
That most people would adore
He is renowned in Harlem and has an affable personality
Selling books, DVDs, clothes and records are his cornerstones of reality
He has marketing skills that only a chosen few possess
In terms of the quality and quantity of his products, he ranks high above the rest
Just like the invisible wind, he makes hard to find albums a reality
Just like a torrential rain fall, folks from all walks of life flock to him to find
Their treasured prize

Call him the Record Man & more laughing and talking in a style that most folks
Would adore
Regardless of the cacophony in the atmosphere, nothing will disturb his rhythm, because
His focus is satisfying his customers
From Count Basie, Billie Holiday, Frank Sinatra, Aretha Franklin, Whitney Houston to
James Brown, you want it – he has it

Books from James Paterson to Richard Wright
You can tell by the look in his eyes, he enjoys the fruit of his endeavor
You can vividly see by the movement of his feet his heart is satisfied when
His customers leave with immense satisfaction written on their faces

Call him the Record Man & More socializing and trying to stay afloat in a complex
World that most of us would really adore

Diagnosis Poetry

Hold me and tell me your most paramount dreams
Make love to me when it does not matter

Kiss me when you know it's the most difficult task to accomplish
Think of me when your world has been overwhelmed by chaos
Write me a poem even though you are not a Poet

Paint a picture of me even though you are not an artist
Surprise me with a gift when a holiday is a mile away
Make me laugh even though you are not a comedian

Show your love just as quick as the days melt to nights
Just imagine how great everything would be If------

Shhhhh-for a Moment

I hear the music and the rhythm telling me we should be together
We should not hold back the tears of yesterday's emotions

Don't let what we have accumulated together fall down on the precipice
Of a faulty discourse

Don't worry about the hush that is still in your heart
What we have will be a bright desideratum for generations to come

The feedback from the wind has blown in a direction that cannot be reversed
Once things are assimilated in the cortex of your mind –it doesn't matter what
Was exposed

Life will continue on and so will we when the atmosphere of LOVE gathers
Stars into the oasis of our hearts

Sonnet In Motion

Talking reality-visualizing artistic endeavor casting away all
The wrongful dirt

Come and discover my world and text away all of the hurt

I want to grab your feelings and toss them deep up into the sky

But before they descend to perfection-you will want to ask me why

E-mailing, texting, face booking-make them turn your world blue

Let us connect and make our destiny come true

They say love is hot, spicy, and complex under the scattering rain

But if we mesh our feelings together-we won't need morphine
To help ease away the pain

I see life –you feel life on the other side of this song

Happiness, heartaches, disappointments, yes sometimes our most
Beloved creatures are better off being left alone

Silently walking – overtly texting enjoying the rapid pace
Metamorphosis of today

I refuse to lay waste my power and have it any other way

I feel the thoughts and ideas circulating through my brain

There were signs of earth calling events milking away the distilling
Rain

Still here under the sub aqueous sea calm on this marvelous earth

Hearing the explosive sounds of the Voices of Reality especially
At childbirth

May thy art and aesthetic behavior seem so surreal

Owning up to the debt we owe each other, let us walk carefully
Through this life together and cement the DEAL

Sounds 1

I'm embedded into you with everlasting eternity
My bones vibrate when you stimulate my dorsal channel
The scenery of you keeps the folks in direct passage of the wonderful world
Of yesterday's memories
The nerves in my system get so aroused when I ascertained that the novelty of you
Has been created by another individual
I master and master and receive the same prolific feedback
I often wonder about your inherent expressed evolutions
You enter into ones blood vessels in day light and in darkness
When attending a social function, your overpowering statements leave ones social
System in complete satisfaction
From Frank Sinatra, Nat King Cole, Michael Jackson to James Brown
From Billie Holiday, Aretha Franklin, Whitney Houston to Beyoncé, you have left
Your indelible trademarks on this universe
It's interesting to note that the introverts and extroverts cling to you at contrasting times
You are deeply immersed in the ubiquitous Motown sound

I get all choked up when I hear you in the wonderful Stax sound
You bring out the best in people's feelings when they listen to the great Philly sound
When you want to dance and escape from your worries, there is nothing like the
Prolific James Brown sound
You are impromptu in many unique aspects
You have been known to put folks in their selective moods with your high ladder of cleverness

From way back when to the present time, people still enjoy and simply cannot get enough
Of you
Memorable Sounds you make them attain their ultimate orgasms, when you unwind your
Enthralling and diverse elements

The Changing Scenes of Life

The impatient wind danced and swirled to the youthful stars in
Proximity
The world was young, energetic, and the beautiful atmosphere depicted
A rhythm of verve and vigor
Just like a wild beast in human nature, life was standing on the mountain
Top of their dreams
They held the world in the palm of their hands
The face of life wore a handsome smile that had no equal
Their hearts beat to the sounds of ambition and determination
The clock was moving, but destination was infinite
They danced with the times and their steps marched with peerless precision
They saw tomorrow all wrapped up in the spirit of today
Years moved on changing the reflections in the atmosphere
They did not succumb to the tempting vulnerabilities,
But kept up with the vacillating scenes
As challenges surfaced, they were met with uncanny resolve
They looked around and discerned a generational shift in rhythm and attire
At times there were separation in their lives, but it was music to their
souls when they were able to rebound and connect again
The scenes of life continued to change, but the love and respect they had
for each other could not be added in a mathematical equation
As the scenes of life continued to change, they talked, laughed, and
Reminisced about the blissful events way back when, but stayed afloat
And changed gracefully with the scenes

The Best

During the infant stage of 1989, a group of diverse talented softball players assembled
In a familiar atmosphere
Their main objective was to infiltrate and circumvent a dynasty from continuing, and
Not succumb to trepidation of fear
The manager synthesized a team that was punctuated with speed and power
The line up was pregnant with prolific hitters from beginning to the end
The manager intrinsically knew that his team would ultimately win
The team was able to surmount all obstacles when accosted face to face
Time after time, they were able to fight off their adversaries and remained in the race
Periodically, there was a power shortage, and the manager had only enough players
To field, but when he did the players proved to the world that they were real

The players never succumbed- they kept on displaying resiliency again and again
They inherently knew that one day they would eventually win
At times the offense was phenomenal, and the pitching was unforgettable, which
Uniquely separated them from the rest
When night relinquished to darkness, they proved to the world they were the best
The manager had to methodically plot and experiment with a line up metamorphosis
From time to time
He wanted to manifest to the other teams that attaining the championship was incessantly
On his mind
News had rapidly disseminated that those guys were going to choke again
But like a whirlwind of pandemonium, the crucial games they had to win

They worked laboriously and changed their habits just to place themselves above the rest
They did all the little tangible things to win so they could be called the best
Some players went on to garner individual honors that distinctively propelled them
Above the rest

With strong support from the avid fans, the post victory celebration was characterized
By laughter, joy, and rapturous human excitement
Even in a state of exaltation, they explicably outshined the rest
As the season melted away into the aftermath of reality, they had vividly outplayed the rest

Like a river flowing great sentiments of human nature, in 1989 they were unequivocally
The BEST

The Destroyer

It was a rather strong frigid day in June when a tall handsome young man entered the
Restaurant with a basketball under his right arm
The basketball immediately grabbed his attention
There was a time he made that basketball sing sweet music to his soul

He carefully scrutinized the scenery and the incomparable "Destroyer" decided to join his friend
For brunch
Their conversations vacillated from topic to topic, but basketball became the domineering subject
A well-dressed teenager yelled to his friend "there is the Destroyer over there, my mother showed me newspaper clippings of him, he was a playground legend in Harlem years ago"
He was cool but acknowledged the teenager with a big wide smile
During his era, he was the King of the Rucker tournaments

He had laboriously worked to hone his conspicuous basketball skills
He was cognizant of the realization that to beat the best you had to be the Best
A deep penetrating look in his eyes depicted the ostentatious legacy he had left behind
He played no High school or college basketball
He was endowed with a talent that was almost beyond compare

He played against the All Americans in college and the best that the professional world had
To offer, and was impervious and excelled beyond human comprehension
The Rucker tournament was his home---it was his sanctuary
It was a place he took his vendetta out on his adversaries
When he played, he sent his fans on a wave of mind shocking thrills with his prodigious dunks
And unmatched scoring out bursts

Game after game he would put on a shooting clinic that left fans paralyzed in a state of exultation
On one occasion, he showed up late and still poured in 74 points
His adversaries tried to neutralize his on court floor acumen but fell short
An older man recognized him and hollered out "Destroyer pound for pound you were
The greatest to play in the Rucker's league"
His facial expression acknowledged the sentiment
Time suddenly started to melt the afternoon away
His friend asked him –how would you fare against the best players in basketball today?
He cracked a watermelon smile and said "there are a lot of talented players today, but I still
Would be one step ahead of all of them"
The Incomparable "Destroyer" exited the environment laughing

The Indefatigable Freedom Fighter

From the deep soil of the land, it cast a huge shadow on its inhabitants
It was transpicuous as the atoms and molecules embedded in the earth
Apartheid was a giant demon shattering the moral fiber of a great country

As the situation became more intensified, the indefatigable Freedom Fighter began
To grapple with that viable demon head on
He was strong and fearless and worked laboriously to eradicate the evil of apartheid
Regardless of all the negatives obstacles and challenges he was confronted with daily,
He never succumbed to the relentless external pressure
He was a bright shining star breaking through the dark clouds of injustice
Seeking justice and freedom for his people, he experienced a host of trials and tribulations

During his incarceration, they tried to crush his spirit, but his inner strength and resolve
Only accelerated his momentum
He was ostracized into another hemisphere where hard labor and negative conditions
Became his close companions
He tackled adversity head on gaining indomitable energy from out pouring love from family
And his people
The weapons he used were not firearms or other acts of evil
The weapons he utilized were laborious struggles, unforgettable human sacrifice and overt forgiveness

He fought for a cause and if necessary would die for it
He knew that a man cannot rest on his laurels, but with grit, determination and relentless will power change will surface

He experienced hardships, struggles, separation, but had that conspicuous umbilical cord that
Tied him to his people
He was aware that if people can learn to hate and if that pendulum continues to rotate they can be taught to love

His foes though he would sink in an ocean of quicksand, but like a roaring lion he bounced back
And became President of his country
He drove his nation from the curse of apartheid to a multiracial democracy
Some people change fragment of society, but he transformed South Africa
He had a thirst for equality--- he had a hunger for freedom
He was a beacon of integrity, rectitude and reconciliation
He is gone but his spirit and legacy will live forever

The weapons he used were laborious struggles, Unforgettable human sacrifice and overt
Forgiveness
I look over the hemisphere of South Africa and I hear cacophony sounds from its people shouting
"Madiba we love you and we are going to miss you"
I see the atoms and the molecules conflating
He was loved, admired and cherished by all
President Nelson Mandela thanks for elevating our spirits and changing the World

The King & Company

Just before the season commenced, he had a prolific reverie
The team would accomplish something that had never happened before
History would be made in an exciting fashion in 2016
He woke up smiling promising to make that unforgettable dream a reality

They started the season in a winning mode with an optimistic outlook on their faces
They had built up a strong team spirit and became a cohesive unit
Players were now healthy
His heart and mind had an intercourse with him like never before

Being the best player on the planet, he was constantly under attack, but with
His grit and indefatigable work ethics, he could handle the pressure
He had won nearly every conceivable award on earth, but there was still a big void
He had returned home for a reason
He told his ardent fans they were going to bring that championship trophy to Cleveland

There were doubters, greedy skeptics, and negative feedback, but he was cognizant
Of his God given abilities, and did not let things disturb his mental equilibrium

He knew with his supporting cast, he had enough talent to accomplish his goal
The atmosphere was in a state of frenzy as the two best teams would vie for the crown
He knew that to be the best you had to beat the best
A hush was in the air as they quickly fell behind 3-1
With the title on the line, he knew it was time for him to put his fingerprints on the game

He proved to the world that he was best in class by electrifying the crowd with unbelievable
Three points shots and ambidextrous points to the basket
The seventh game had arrived, and the world was waiting in suspense
They were playing an elite team saturated with talented players, but they were up for
The challenge

At different stages of the game, the unequaled King carried his team on his massive
Shoulders to ensure that victory was imminent
He gave everything he had blood, sweat and tears highlighted by a triple double
To garner the big prize

The coaching staff was masterful in synthesizing various strategies to produce great results
They made history by bringing a championship to the city of Cleveland
The post-game celebration was punctuated by organic pandemonium, and action
Packed bliss

The "King" & Company put a smile on the city of Cleveland that will last forever
When the greatest player of all time is mentioned in a conversation, you will find
LeBron James smiling in the mix

The Marshall Doctrine

The purpose of the paramount keys below is to build character socially as well as academically
It should be perused daily until it becomes a working variable in your life

Develop a positive attitude toward learning and mastering challenging assignments

Set high personal objectives and don't be placated until they are attained
Don't settle or be complacent with average grades
Remember anyone can be mediocre

Be cognizant of what the instructor is saying and ask pertinent questions when the material seems alien or fuzzy

For developmental and intellectual growth, peruse a plethora of sources on a regular basis
During your reading adventures look up words that are not comprehensible

Surround yourself with highly ambitious motivated students

Work laboriously each day to improve socially as well as academically
Examine your weakness and build to strengthen them immediately

Develop great organizational and penmanship skills to complement other existing skills

Develop strong confidence in your ability to succeed in any endeavor regardless of its magnitude
Abstain from peers who indulge in bad habits, and who walk around with their minds filled with pessimism

Maintain a high self-esteem at all times

Watch television shows that are educational, arouse the imagination, and stimulate the intellect

Become a voracious reader, to broaden your score, to better understand the social behavior of others, and to completely comprehend the universe around you and its complexions

Select a career path and devote all energies to it so that maximum results can be attained

Always be true to yourself or others will be false to you

To increase your knowledge of God, learn, read and saturate your mind with information relative to the bible

The Spirit In Your Voice

When I am alone and it feels like the whole world has collapsed on my mind
When I am worried and I cannot seem to unravel the existing quagmire

When I am down and out and it just seems like I cannot take another step
When a multitude of problems and situations are tossed in my direction and I just can't
Seem to grapple with them

When at times it feels like there is no answer to a specific need
When at times it just seem like I cannot make it through the day

But when I relax my mind and get my thoughts together
I know I will get the desired results when I hear IT

I listen to IT and suddenly the storms in life have quickly vanished
My world is in an atmosphere of tranquility
Because of IT I am at peace with the world and more importantly I am at peace
With my self

Oh sweet, powerful SPIRIT ----if you were not omnipresent I would be lost

The Unequaled Air Jordan

He first arrived at the professional level without anyone hardly knowing his name
But before very long, he began to prove to the world that he was on his way to Fortune and fame
He grabbed and captured his fans with his extraordinary leaping abilities in the air
Making unbelievable baskets
At times he flies like a bird and leaps like a giraffe scoring points leaving his defenders
In unshakeable clouds of total confusion

He leads his team in leadership and spiritual motivation, and when it's time to win
A game, he comes through with his own unique creation
Teams try all sorts of strategies to shut his game down, but he accelerates to a higher
Level of achievement gaining new fans from miles around
He is a legend- he is an icon, and he is a man called Air
He is ubiquitous on the basketball court striking fear in his defender's mind
Every time he touches the ball
He is the fiercest competitor on the court today, and when it comes to winning
The game, he always makes certain that his team arise to the top forbidding
Anything to stand in the way
He plays with such intensity and defies all odds that he leaves his team mates
And adversaries in a state of awe
With a strong winning attitude showing on his countenance, and utilizing acrobatic moves
In the air to score a three pointer, that onlookers can barely believe what they saw
Night after night lifting the screaming crowd to its feet with his display of superior
Athletic ability, heroics and conspicuous court acumen

Air Jordan hanging the air paralyzing his opponents so that he can magnificently culminate
Another incredible basket as pandemonium takes the stadium hostage
The indefatigable Air Jordan rising from his sick bed in a state of conspicuous weariness
Displaying resiliency punctuated by a high degree of intensity crushing his opponents,
With a game winning shot at the buzzer as the crowd goes wild in an orgasm of excitement

Winning almost every conceivable award and setting new records, and lifting his team to
Consecutive championships, yet he is vying to surpass all previous accomplishments

As the game clock makes its destination toward the end of the game, the unequaled Air
Jordan will be making another sensational game winning shot with sea of opponents in his face,
To the joy and rapture of his most ardent fans

There were Chamberlain, West, Magic, Bird, The big O, Dr J and all of the rest, but when you
Look in the sports dictionary and look up Jordan it will say during his era he was the BEST

The Wanderer

She sat in the restaurant trying to hold off the sweltering heat wave and suddenly noticed him
She had seen him before partaking in his daily ritual
The humidity was oppressive, but it did not disturb his rhythm
He wore a watermelon smile on his countenance and his headset was in the proper place

Passersby strolled by him revealing scant attention
Regardless of the season, he did not alter his most treasured habit
Occasionally, he would hear a voluptuous voice, but it did not faze him
The cacophony in the surrounding milieu did not matter, because he was lost in his own world
He would slightly elevate his speed when he heard one of James Brown's signature songs
"I feel good"

He looked friendly, but was conspicuously laconic
Each movement was characterized by uncanny precision as he continued to roam
He was a Wanderer fast pacing from block to block
He was a wanderer and he visibly did it nonstop
She hurriedly swallowed her food and egressed the congested environment
She peaked in her rear view mirror and he was still pacing back and forth

Time suddenly started to eat the afternoon away, but he continued to pace
Suddenly four young men passed by him and one of them nearly knocked him to the pavement
He looked up and noticed that their pants were almost kissing the pavement
He did not utter a word, but shame and disgust were depicted in his eyes
He whispered to himself "Young men why- Young men why", but continued to pace

The heat intensified and cold sweat covered his face like clothes on one's body
She was farther away now looking into her periphery vision reflected a man immersed
In the ambition of his dreams

Tomorrow Is Another Day

I am having my troubles now, but I won't let them stand in my way
I am a true faith believer, because tomorrow is another day
Right now, nothing seems to be going my way
But I am not going to give up, because tomorrow is another day

I've got to hold on to my decisions and ambitions
I've got to keep on until everything turns to abundant fruition
I will keep on pushing until there is some light ahead
I just won't rest another night in bed
I will keep on trying in every possible way
Because tomorrow is another day—yes tomorrow is another day
Tomorrow could bring a few heartaches and pain, or it could shower me
With a lot of luck
But people you can bet that I will never give up
Some people may tell me that I should just give up and quit
But in no way I will be like them and just give up on life and sit
I will keep moving on and may find the true facts of life the hard way
But baby I am a firm believer in the good things to come
Because tomorrow is another day--yes, it's another day

I will never stop until I reach that mountain top
You see I always believe that one day something good will come my way
That's why I say tomorrow is another day
Deep down in my heart and soul, I can see something positive is out there for me
One of these good old days something good will be coming my way
I will keep on pushing regardless of what they say
I just can't stop now—I must hold on to my dreams and aspirations
I am not going to be beset by hardships and tribulations

Because tomorrow is another day
My almighty Creator will always provide
Yes, baby tomorrow is another DAY

Violence Eradicated

It's time to look into the mirror of your soul
It's time to make negative behavior history
Listen closely to your heart beat
It should be beating to the drum of a new attitude
It should be beating to the drum of a brand new you
That heart beat should be beating to the sound of I will make a difference

You must commit yourself to eliminate those dangerous Land Mines from your
Ideology
It's time to look and listen to the world around you
See the negatives and surmount them with the positives
Stand up and persevere with conspicuous interesting rectitude
Don't get swallowed up by undesirable situations and social conditions
Be the role model that YOU will marvel at
Too many of our young are being killed

Plant the seed to your soul and make that seed blossom into superior academic
Upward mobility
Don't get turned on by false images
Don't get lulled by false prophets

Too many of our young are being killed without having the opportunity to
Achieve their ambition in life

It's time to coalesce and ferret out negative activities
We must stop the violence now
Violence must be eradicated
It is rupturing the moral essence of our communities
It is eating away at the raw core of our dreams
We must love each other in a mode that will set a positive example for the world
Let the world see us in a different bright light

Let's put self respect back on the dinner table
Let's walk with pride, dignity and elevated self esteem that will go unchallenged
And be highlighted by steppingstones of greatness
It is time to open your eyes to a great sun shine of tomorrow and not to a
Constipation of moral decay
Let you behavior speak high volumes of satisfaction and admiration and build
Up a healthy alliance for tomorrow
Make self-motivation and determination the main source of your menu
Stand up and be a positive voice
Be a voice that your family, friends and the world will rave about
Stand up and make an impact
Begin to create a positive legacy that the world will cherish and remember
Let your thoughts sour high like the clouds in the sky
Let your ambitions run wild like the stars at night
As you profoundly ponder your future and the future of others- make certain that
You pregnant your mind with Love, Life and more importantly GOD

So my friends-----------Violence must be eradicated
Ask not what your community can do for you, but from the moral essence of your
Being ask yourself what positive contributions will I immediately begin to make for the betterment of my community
We all must work together
VIOLENCE MUST BE ERADICATED

Waiting

Stop and search your mind, heart and soul
Just let me get to know you—don't remain a stranger

Can't you feel our love circulating in unison in the air
Frequent text messages and sending love poetic cards simply will not get the job done

You said you did not want a platonic relationship
Trust yourself, but more importantly trust me we can make it together

Come and let us explore each other
Come and let us discover this mysterious universe together

We can write our own prescription for life and it does not have to be approved by a physician

Baby wash out the rain and bring in the beautiful sun
Let go of those stubborn defense mechanisms and come trophy angel into a happy home of love
Sometimes patience wears thin as a string of spaghetti over a period

Waiting in vain is just like a disappearing act

Baby I don't want to wait in vain
Please don't let me wait in vain

Wheel of life

We travel down and up many roads in life in circulatory fashion
We must stay on the right course or immediately our destination will be derailed

As we are spinning around, we are confronted by the inevitable Wheel of Life drawn
Together under a mask of disguise at times

The world is watching you with piercing eyes and analyzing you with transparent thoughts
The world will hear you as the tracks of your footsteps render a deep rooted testimony

As your world turns will you be consumed by jealously, greed, avaricious behavior fortified by promiscuous exhibitions
Regardless as to how the wheel moves, you must remain resilient with unwavering strength
Of moxie

In that dark desert of your sphere, sinful ways and negative preoccupations will sever your heart and soul

Open your heart and mind to help and applaud others as they receive their long over due
Goodness in life and your attachment to the wheel will go unchallenged and remain strong

The wheel is a continuous cycle and based on your feelings and motivations, you must stay afloat and those beautiful abundant blessings will be yours

Don't become a FUGITIVE to your own soul and remain inside, because you will be swallowed up by swirling elements of quicksand
Even when the Wheel shifts like blowing snow, you must let your actions sow seeds of righteousness and justice

Challenging life events will continue at unpredictable times, but where will your heart, mind, and soul rest?

Write A Poem For Me

I can tell by the way you walk showing all your beauty, so the world can see
Nothing would satisfy me more than if you would write a poem for me
I know you have feelings that you have never shared before
Tell me your thoughts share your most clandestine emotions via twitter or text Write a poem for me- come on baby write a poem for me
It can be as penetrating, timeless as the "Voices of Reality"
Mixing it from side to side- exploring a theme that you never should hide
Describing the beauty of human nature that some have left behind
Highlighting the laughter between the two oak trees
Reminiscing about the sands of time and making a mockery out of the Birds and bees
Come on and write a poem for me
It can be Saturated with the same concoctions as "Voices of Reality"
You have the style, intellect, creativeness and personality
I know you can satisfy my inner thirst feeling that wonderful aubade early One morning
Tap into the wonders of this massive universe
Adding and multiplying the theories of revelation
Tap into the reservoir of your soul, enjoying the youthful experience
Never contemplating growing old
Come on let me experience the cadence and the rhythm of your thoughts
You are a talented raconteur -just want to glean a little of your philosophy
So, come on and write a poem for me

Dreaming Plus

I dreamed about you last night
It was the most beautiful dream I have ever had
Your smile was great, and your conversation was constipated with sexual overtones
We made love in a mysterious place pregnant with historic meaning
We made future plans as the snowflakes had their own social intercourse together
We did not call one another by name, but our soul spirits knew all those vivid details

I dreamed about you last night
I was overwhelmed by your natty dress mode and loving fragrance
I could not wake up from the sweet reverie, because you would not let me
The snow quickly changed to a picturesque rain

I wonder did you ever dream about me
It would be hard to comprehend or ascertain as we have never met

The phantasmagoric events were difficult to understand
I dreamed about you very long last night
Yes, I dreamed about you last night

Incomparable Poet

(For Langston Hughes)

Folk's ideas were disseminated all over this universe, when you decided to show the world your seminal talents
We were searching and seeking for a new poetic voice and you quickly accelerated to the top
Like cream in coffee
You wrote at a time when we desperately needed your incomparable expression
You depicted in your marvelous works-daily testimonies that will go unchallenged and
Will remain cemented in TIME
People all over this universe have admired and cherished your creative endeavors
Your seminal works soothe the soul like the blessing sunshine warms ones heart
The themes, similes and metaphors you utilized in your poetry will never be erased from
My cerebrum

Oh Langston! Oh Langston! You wrote with such passion and fervor that the arteries in my Blood told their own unique stories
Your renowned poems revealed times and places I still see, feel and smell in my dreams
You hypnotized and baptized the world with your poems of praise, love and other social
Conditions

When I think of your poems "Harlem", "The Negro speaks of rivers", my mind just escapes into
A world of drum beating ecstasy
What you have left to the world will never be duplicated again
You are no longer with us, but I still feel and hear your whispers in the deep valley of my soul

During your generation and today, your footprints on fellow writers will never be replaced
When I read your work, you arouse my imagination and creativity nearly beyond human
Comprehension
When I think of words that light my fire—I think of YOU
When I mull over words that relax my mind and spirit, your infectious poetry comes
Running to my mind

As people on this planet march on to their destinations, and Poets continue to grapple with their own feelings, in the background of my conscious when I think of poetry and its
Consequences –Langston! oh Langston Hughes, I will continue to contemplate
Your greatness

Operation HOPE Poem

They come to Operation HOPE from many diverse locations
They all come to Operation HOPE sometimes with complex financial situations
They come after finding out there is no other place to go
Others come mainly due to the Chairman's prolific social discourse on the TV and radio
Some live in close proximity and others live far away
Just as sure as darkness melts to light, the come to Operation HOPE every single day

They come seeking economic advice and positive direction
They come in large crowds, because they have a voracious appetite to partake in an education
Seminar
From the North, South, East and mostly everywhere, people are serious about their financial
Situation, and come in for credit repair
All over the globe, they come in seeking advice on how to write a business plan
Snow is falling- rain is pouring down- the sun is shining-the Wind is making a screaming noise,
They rush in as fast as they can
The young come for Financial empowerment, Financial literacy programs and internet access
They come with scant knowledge regarding the road to success,
But end up taking the Silver Rights road to Entrepreneurship
When they add and multiply all of the services deep down in their hearts, they know they are receiving the best

Some are frightened, confused and their psychological state is pregnant with trepidation and doubt
But they are quickly relieved and satisfied when they understand what Operation HOPE is all about
They come anxiously with family members and friends

Out of sheer curiously, others come proudly on their own with dangling business ideas pregnant in their minds
People flock to Operation HOPE in search of a business loan
Oh, but when they depart it's a different story
When they leave, you can discern a world of satisfaction written on their faces
When the leave, you can hear the sound of joy and a sense profound happiness in their voices
When they depart, one can see a clear visible metamorphosis in their personalities and an elevated self esteem

Some are struggling with personal issues and others are enjoying excellent health
A lot of Clients attend all of the seminars, because they know they will be on the road to
Building wealth

With due diligence, perseverance and the way life can change with an unexpected stroke
Be it Computer and Internet access, start a business, obtain a business or mortgage loan, hone your budgeting skills, Foreclosure prevention, Banking on our Future, 5 million Kids initiative

The doors are always open and the hard working dedicated staff will always have faith and be ready like the changing weather at Operation HOPE

Godfather of Soul

The music world was looking and was hungry and thirsty for someone new, different, exciting and explosive
Just like cloudiness turns into sunshine, He arrived

Since the inception of music there have been a host of talented entertainers who have come and vanished into thin air

There are only a select few who have stood the test of time

When you chew up and digest it all- there was one unique, gifted, talented and consummate entertainer who had maintained that staying power and defied all odds
When you think about soul music that will make you feel good
When you are ill-music that will make you want to dance, and if you are lost in a dream

When you think about music that will be always present, and give you a new scent of life
His music will come flying to your mind

As you take a deep breath and consolidate all of those components together, the final output will be the Hardest Working Man in Show Business

Watching him perform over the years, his ardent fans were amazed, spellbound, and caught up in a frenzy of breathing excitement

As time marched on, the Hardest Working Man in Show Business continued to package a revue that was unequaled in style, creativity and precision

Other performers all over the universe have tried to emulate his musical sound and dance creativity, but continue to conspicuously fall short
They will try imitating, but will never duplicate

Yes, he is gone but not forgotten
The Godfather of Soul mixed Jazz, Soul, Blues and Funk still catapulted the gregarious crowd to complete ecstasy and fulfillment after each song was performed

Each new show was punctuated with sustained energy – new eye catching creativity, and overall unparalleled showman ship acumen that will go unchallenged

With such renowned signature songs like "Please Please", "Papa Got A Brand New Bag", "Cold Sweat", "It's A Man's World", "I Feel Good", "Living In America" and many great others, the indefatigable entertainer continued to thrill, excite, tease and ultimately satisfied his adoring fans right through his FINAL performance

Regardless of all the fame, fortune and plethora of awards, the versatile singer continued to give a high-octane performance sliding, spinning, dancing and catapulting his legion of fans into a state of paroxysmal excitement

When the last musical raindrop is carefully analyzed, standing tall and never forgotten will be the originator of soul music the incomparable, unrivaled Mr. James Brown

IT (Coronavirus)

It is a small word, but can have a ginormous impact on the world
It has saturated the social media in unmatched fashion
It has become an invisible enemy leaving its trademarks in a mode we
Have not witnessed before
All over this massive universe, it is called Coronavirus
It is a virus that has disrupted lives, and the economy in unspeakable terms
It has deeply wounded the moral fiber of this universe
Its so deadly the President had to call for a state of national emergency
The psychological impact can be conspicuously seen in daily social intercourse
Touching and shaking hands have almost become distant cousins
Social distancing has become a luminous reality
It is metastasizing in areas that will go unchallenged
It doesn't discriminate, and shows no compassion
It doesn't care about your race or gender
It is a super enemy and has impacted small and large businesses

As the days pass on, millions have contracted the virus, and many have Succumbed to death
Without a doubt, the world is in a vicious war with an invisible enemy
It has quickly and drastically changed the standard of living among the masses
We are living in what is now called "The New Normal"
Social distancing and Repetitive hand washing have become marriage partners
Big whispers in the air are saying that romance has taken a back seat to social distancing
It has caused isolation and fear
People are in a vise of fear, panic, and trepidation grappling with the reality that they
Might have it, or the next person they encounter might have it
In the background of my mind, I hear a record-breaking song called "Social distancing and Frequent

Hand washing"
I hear racing up the charts in second place another song called "You better wear your mask"
It has merged people together in a quick and disturbing manner and simultaneously
Separated families in unimaginable ways
To a great degree, we are now living in a Mask oriented world
You can tell by the way people communicate, they are afraid
You can tell by the look in their eyes, people are profoundly concerned
During this global pandemic just contemplate what the psychological state the world would
Be in, if we did not have cell phones

Looking through the clouds, we are beginning to make a big comeback
We are vigilant, strong, resilient and have profound fortitude to surmount all challenges
Just as certain as the sun will rise tomorrow, the invisible enemy will be DEFEATED

On up that unpredictable road, when you look up Coronavirus in the medical dictionary
It will say IT

BJ

He first made his appearance on the field back in the early part of May to play for a softball team called CPSAA
I did not know him well until he arrived at bat
Vividly emblazoned on the back of his uniform were the letters BJ

As soon as the season progressed, he conspicuously became flexible and loose
Every game he has played in, he has certainly produced

Standing on the sideline, he works laboriously and leads his team in motivation
And when he accosts the plate, his style is characterized by fierce concentration

He told me "All I see before my viable vision is a championship for CPSAA"
People the man I am talking about is the Matchless BJ
When he is not playing, the tempo of the game is not the same
Especially when his man Tex isn't calling out his name

When he steps to the plate, the indefatigable Jones gives CPSAA all that he can give
The team knows that something positive is going to happen when his ardent fan Tex yells out "Hey BJ show them where you live"
Sometimes when melancholy surrounds the players and they feel they are going to lose at home
Like a sudden bomb explosion BJ belts out "Come on you all let's get it on"
When he plays, his output is always 100 percent
When one profoundly probes his softball stats, he ascertains the man is leading the club in every pertinent department
He is an incredible athlete in every conceivable way
When it comes to natural inherent talent, there is no one quite like BJ

When out in a social atmosphere, one finds him engaged in an animated
conversation, because he always has something paramount to say
People find the setting punctuated by laughter, bliss, and joy when they
are in the company of the Incomparable BJ

This poem has come to an end and synthesizing it was raw fun
Realistically speaking, for Bobby Jones the legend has just begun

Mrs. G

She has gone on to be with her Prince of Peace and Creator
She was one of a kind and her overall abilities will go unmatched

I cannot bring to write the imprints she left on my life
Making me realize what work was even before I could hardly utter the word

I still see her in those long sweltering cotton fields
Picking as much cotton as a machine

Never complaining just working at an unbelievable pace
My eyes cry out in tears knowing that she was performing her task
Working with a missing limb
She beautifully limned to me a picture of life I cannot describe

I still see her face and hear her voice
A voice and message that will live forever
She invented the phrase "Never give up on life"

Whenever I feel I am at the nadir point of life
I suddenly discern a positive metamorphosis in my life
Simply because I think of her

That Special Day

Before that day arrived, I had dreamed hard and long about it
It would be a day like no one had ever experienced
It would not be duplicated again

After so many years of contemplation and procrastination, I knew I had to fulfill that lucid dream

As the days and months ticked away, I could feel that inherent decision sweeping closer to my heart and thought apparatus

Relatives will meet and celebrate for the first time on that special day
People from every conceivable ethnic group and educational background will surface on that day

As the day grew nearer, the surrounding walls to my veins in my body began to make the proper connections

An event cannot happen until the heart, mind and other attaching cells are dancing in unison to the same rhythm
Nothing reaches its fruition until the last raindrop has reached its destination

All the growing euphoria will be added and multiplied on that day

As the road to success is standing on the calendar of time, the true psychological mind must wonder at times why did it take so long to attain the greatest bliss of life

Finally, the past became present and that Special Day had become reality

The Dancer Becomes The Poet

The temptation was unbearable, and he was quickly losing touch with reality
The long dolorous looking cigarette dropped unnoticed on the floor
Yes the temptation was getting a lot hotter
Strong sexual desires were growing

The sultry shaped ubiquitous dancer was working laboriously her two sumptuous hookers widely on the dingy bandstand
Two more glasses of white label on the rocks, and the ego was completely elated

The sexy eyes of the vivacious go-go girl had suddenly started a huge chain reaction
The viable energetic music put the super ego in its proper perspective

The unequivocal message she was sending started a careful scrutiny of what was to come
The almost nude body had made perspiration ascend down the face like a tide talking in an animated ocean debate
The profound consumption of alcohol had universally played its role
AS others achieved immense enjoyment in other social spheres of life, he was in his own heterogeneous universe of social intercourse and satisfaction, and no one could disturb his pattern

He then turned around aimlessly and walked out of the ecstatic but heated milieu with a paucity of change, and a world of exciting memories

Remembering Ferguson

As I remember back into the sanctuary of my soul, I think about and profoundly
Miss you---------We had a long stable bond

When I think about you –I think of all the joy and happiness you brought to others,
When you were working in your field of endeavor
Your love and compassion for others will go unmatched

I remember the host of places in this universe we frequented—the people we met
And the activities we shared

Over the years at my athletic events and various award ceremonies- regardless of the weather,
Social commitments, health status –you were always there
I could always depend on you

At times when others would vanish into thin air—you were there
As I cite these few words, I am unable to see you, but I know that you are present, because
I can feel your spirit

I hear that great voice of reality still telling me "Hey man you can do it"

In sum, I have no feeling of melancholy—I don't feel lugubrious

I know that your Creator has called you home and all is ok now
So my Dear brother as the rest of us continue to grapple with the daily challenges
Of life ---may your soul rest in peace

God bless you

Unborn Poem

You have arrested my attention to the degree that at times my thought process feels like its frozen in time

I want to bring you to surface, but I cannot locate the words in my vocabulary to depict you

I made love to you until you almost achieved paroxysmal excitement, but you remained dormant

If I could somehow deliver you from the mirror of my mind, then the entire world would have an opportunity to voice an opinion

I often wonder how you would truly measure up to your peers

I can feel you constantly growing in character and popularity

I deeply ponder will I admire, idolize and love you tomorrow as much as I do today

Deep inside I know one day my curiosity will be completely placated, because that will be the day when you finally emerge and be born

Soundless Tracks

He searched his mind knowing all the time he could note erase the social residue from his conscious

He was told to exercise his abilities to get in touch with reality

Faced with a world that was cold, thirsty, savorless, overpowering and punctuated by massive warnings- he thought he could conquer all

Over and over again he saw naked faces of reality ride his ideas down an obscure path to a giant wave of doom

He tried seeking other social avenues, but was greeted by old man difficulty He tried to attain domestic stability, but that lingering trademark of yesterday was too vivid and omnipotent

His profound lust for other vices led him further into a raw universe of scarcity

Significant others wanted him to shift gears in a novel positive mode, but his world was constipated with the get rich quick schemes

As the elements of society splashed hard up against the walls of destiny, he was grappling with razor sharp ideas hoping that perhaps the next adventure will have a modicum of success

As another old idea plastered against his opinion, his eyes suddenly closed with the hope of opening to a better and brighter future

Babe

Your excellent intensity
    unravels my cerebrum

The highness of your laughter
    excites my lower environment

Your shining delights catch me
    in the correct stage of my essence

Your contacts move with
such elastic desperation

Superficial darkness
    Widens my unique desires

The blended structure
    of your delight inner visions
    touches me
    with a drastic solution

Some how I can feel
    solutions penetrate
    to the top of my threshold

Erroneous facts make me quiver
    in complete blissful evidence
    but the overture
    is still
    an everlasting
    goal

A Misunderstanding

A misunderstanding can turn a sunny bright day quickly into a gloomy dreary night

A misunderstanding can cause a real relationship to drive down divided paths

It can break your heart when you are trying to bring reconciliation back to surface

At times it has ruptured a friendship beyond repair

It has caused once viable marriages to terminate

A misunderstanding has starved off love when it should have been on the main menu

It has destroyed harmony in the household when a touch of apology would have brought stability to the atmosphere

It has caused friction in this global universe, when just a little understanding, and reasoning would be the perfect therapeutic solution

When we look into the mirror and really examine our inner core with conspicuous
Veracity, then a misunderstanding will become a floating memory of the past

Free

I'm tired of concealing my deep inherent feelings for you
I tried revealing my real feelings for you, but reciprocity was not your favorite cup of tea
I am going to tell the entire world about how I feel
I am going to write about it in the world's most celebrated newspapers
Let them witness it on Facebook

I want the television world to see and feel the impact
I want reality to spread my sweet bliss
I want them to be seen on DVD
Let them see it in a text message
Let them read about it in an e-mail document

Finally, let joy and happiness have their own social discourse

Feeling so much better now – so much better

The Thought Revisited

It simply would not vanish
It was a thought that was greater than any other thought
The thought had been long contemplated even during times when he fancied other crowded pathways of love

He had thrown it out, but it kept coming back at the most visible times
Even during his most prolific sleeping adventures his most vivid reveries were immersed with the thought

When daybreak surfaced, the thought was cemented on his mind
At times it was the most fiendish insinuating thought and there was no escape from it

On the most tempestuous but clearly beautiful evening, it would be standing on his heart

It was cracking and ripping through ever atom of his body
The thought danced with him and it would sing with him

He grappled with the thought, but it would never separate from him

Biden – Build Back Better

He had tried before, but had failed
It was in the moral fiber of his soul, he had to run again
The world was speaking to him clearly and he listened

The world was grappling with one of the deadliest global pandemics in history
The odds were against him, but he decided to run again
Based on what he saw and heard, he decided to run on the theme Build Back Better
He was going to fight for the soul, heart and spirit of the country
He saw a world rupturing in paramount areas

With grit, determination, and strong will power, he ultimately became the democratic
Nominee
He looked out and saw a nation that needed to be healed
He saw a country that needed to be quickly united in a conspicuous mode
Integrity, decency, compassion and empathy were at the top of his menu

Some folks on the right ridiculed him saying he was incompetent, and had
Diminished cognitive skills
It was a tough campaign, but through it all he was unflappable
With due diligence, hard human sacrifice, and unmatched get out to
Vote campaign, he was victorious at the end

He said he was going to be a change agent, and proved it by selecting
The first woman of color Kamala Harris as his Vice President
His inaugural speech was something special focusing on keeping the faith,
Remaining optimistic and hammering on the theme unity cohesion

His administration has a plethora of problems to tackle, a global pandemic, a crippled
Economy, massive unemployment, growing threat of terrorism, racial violence, child

Poverty, infrastructure and other challenging issues
Synthesizing the most diverse cabinet in history, his administration is ready for the challenge
You can tell by the smile on his face, he is happy and blessed to have working with him the
First female VP Kamala Harris

In order to build back better, we need to come together in a cohesive fashion like never
We need to work diligently to defeat this deadly virus so we can ultimately return to a
Normal standard of living

To build back better, we need to work laboriously to create good paying jobs open schools,
Businesses, so people can return to work
We must quickly provide the economic stimulus to people who really need it
Since the new President has been in office, there is a new optimistic spirit swirling
Around in the universe
I look through the clouds and discern a positive psychological metamorphosis in human behavior we are strong, resilient and the mighty invisible Virus will soon be defeated
With the Biden/Harris administration I see problems being solved and conspicuous results
Attained
Based on build back better, we will come back stronger than ever in all pertinent spheres
There will be a wonderful harmony in the air that never existed before
The President and Vice President have diagnosed the gargantuan problems the world
Is facing
Based on build back better, the Biden/ Harris administration will provide the best prescription

The Beautiful Lady In The Subway

He was restless for several nights, because he was haunted by a recurrent dream
A dream depicting that he would meet someone special in the subway
He thought but why in the subway
His romantic life was unraveling, because his partner had terminated their liaison
He had to face another hard day at work
Being a therapist trying to solve other individuals problems can be difficult
The day melted away and he was elated it was Friday
It was a little after 12 AM as he glanced up at the stars
They were flashing in a cohesive rhythm
He received good vibration from the impatient wind as it whistled by
The moon was looking good too
He thought in silence that something good was going to happen for him
He landed down the subway stairs and glanced toward the stationary booth
There she was looking in his direction

The Beautiful Lady In the subway
His heart nearly jumped out of his chest
He first thought it was an apparition – he was paralyzed by her beauty
She was attractive and seemed to have all of the attributes he was seeking
A train had just departed, so it was obvious she was waiting for someone---But who?
He passed by her---their eyes connected, but he continued on
She vacillated between looking in her book, and constantly peaking toward the subway stairs

The dream—the dream there she is right in front of me—The Beautiful Lady In the subway
He tried to catch her attention, but she exhibited no interest
A voice blasted in the air saying the train would be 20 minutes late
He looked and noticed her countenance revealed a state of merriment
There was a happiness in her eyes that a dictionary could not explain

You could tell by the way she paced she was looking forward to forthcoming events
He could tell that she was preoccupied with something
He tried again to attract her attention, but the words would not evacuate

Suddenly she heard a loud whisper --- she marched toward the subway stairs
He was there saying "I am here it's OK now'
She replied "so glad you are here darling lets go"
The train arrived and he stepped inside
He said to an unknown rider "for one brief moment – she made my day
The Beautiful Lady In The Subway----The Beautiful Lady In The Subway

We Are People 2

Now some of us may not be as successful as you
But you must realize that we are people too

Some of us are just as talented and educated as you
Just like the earth is infinite, we are people too
This is our country too, although we are very crowd
There is just a hand full of us, but we are exceedingly proud
You just can't leave us behind
Because we have the same voice and intelligent mind

We have the same legs and arms
We have the same lips and when necessary can turn on the magical charm
You can't forget we like to enjoy the sunshine, and the wonderous blue skies
You can't forget we have the same pair of eyes

Happy people- soulful people- intelligent people- down to earth people
We are people too--- we are people 2
Some of us attain upward mobility just like you
Some of us are just as healthy and wealthy as you

Let's work together to eliminate jealousy and poverty
Let's come together and make racism vanish

When I contemplate what our ancestors had to endure, we must strive for
Excellence in everything we do
Because we are people 2--- we are people too
Keep on pushing until you attain your inherent objective---never surrender
Regardless of your ethnicity or gender
You must maintain your faith in your omnipresent, omnipotent, omniscience God

There is nothing like the power source in you
Let's all work together to change the world in a remarkable fashion

Because we are people too
We Are People 2

Words

I hear them loud and clear busting up against the inner wall of my mind
Big words small words, the world cannot function without them
They can elevate your spirit into another stratosphere
They can drop a big blow to your ego

Words the entire universe is grappling with the impact of words
At times, they can inspire and motivate
Other times, they can yield nothing but heartaches and sorrow
Everyday people scattered around this global universe are making paramount
Decisions based on what they read and hear

They are peripatetic and there is no escape from them
We love them- we cherish them- we would be lost without them
I feel them racing against my most inherent desires and aspirations
They will make you laugh- they will make you cry
They can start a deadly war in a split second, and make you contemplate why

When you are down and out, there is that voice telling you to read the Word, study the Word
When you are struggling with your health, finances, internal family conflicts, you will hear
That booming voices saying "Go to the Word, study the Word – fall in love with the Word"

The entire universe is grappling with the impact of Words
Sooner or later, we will be responding to Words
Some of the GOAT Dr. King, Malcolm X and JFK masterfully articulated them in a
Mode that will forever go unmatched in style and substance
Just like the sun will shine somewhere tomorrow, people will continue to grapple with
The consequences of what they hear and read

Words- Words- Words

I Have Seen Blacks at Work

I have seen them working from sunup to sundown
I have seen them up close and from miles around

I have seen them toiling at various occupations working for less than five dollars
A week
I have seen them working in 100-degree weather almost starving for a simple glass of water
I have seen perspiration roll of their bodies like rain and wind during hurricane
Season

I have seen them glaze up at the sky hoping and praying for inclement weather
So that they could catch a wink of much needed rest

I have seen and heard Blacks at work
I have heard their voices loud and clear

I have seen the pain in their eyes and heard the melancholy in their conversations

There were the voices singing those heartfelt gospel songs and reciting poetry to help ease the tremendous burden on a long laborious day

I have heard the footsteps of hard times each time they would find their paths to those old long wide cotton fields
Planting, hoeing, picking cotton and killing deadly snakes at the same time
Plowing those mules and picking large bales of hay

I have seen blacks at work
I have seen and heard blacks of all ages at work

Women some of them partial disabled carrying babies on their backs while picking as much as two hundred pounds of cotton a day

I have seen them wash tons of clothes a day with their two hands –some with only one hand – the only machine they had were their hands
I have seen men work harder than the word itself just to provide for the survival of their families

Yes, I have seen destitute Blacks at work

Cameron's Ponds

Just the bare facts of thinking about them, my heart becomes full of joy and happiness

They are scattered all over the geographical scene unmatched in competition

They are open for fishing purposes only certain times of the season
Just like a kid with a new toy, I can't wait to visit them

When I view the crystal blue water all the nerves in my body begin to sing sweet music to each other

I look across the vast ponds and immediately see God's universal beautiful creation

People from all over the universe come to fish in those large eye-catching ponds

Everyone is waiting to catch the big trophy fish of the day
Others are just happy to share vicarious memories of the past

Some folks fish there for just short periods, while others simply make it an all-day affair

Once you see those ponds so beautiful in nature that you will always want to return, because the excitement will remain fixed in your mind

The talk of the town is Go to Cameron's Ponds

No other form of sport activity will give you the positive therapeutic results as fishing in Cameron's Ponds

As the days and nights continue to roll on, I will be thinking of those Ponds

About the Author

David A. Marshall is a songwriter/poet. He is the author of the riveting poetry book "Voices of Reality". He was born in York, SC where he graduated from Jefferson High School. He subsequently relocated to New York and continued his education by Graduating from Baruch College majoring in psychology and sociology. Education included one year of graduate studies.

He always had an insatiable appetite for the written word, and has been writing songs and poetry extensively over the last four decades. His writings have garnered a plethora of awards. In his poetry, you will find the soaking up of spirituality, human nature, and the many faces of love, and its consequences.

When he is not reading or writing, he enjoys fishing, watching old movies, watching sports and listening to R & B. His influences include Langston Hughes, Nikki Giovanni, Edgar Allan Poe, Richard Wright and James Baldwin. Before retiring, he was a Certified Financial Counselor for many years. He is working on a novel and resides in Harlem, New York.

CPSIA information can be obtained
at www.ICGtesting.com
Printed in the USA
JSHW081153240323
39413JS00001B/85